Bowling

Sports in Action

in Action

Niki Walker & Sarah Dann
Photographs by Marc Crabtree
⚘ Crabtree Publishing Company

www.crabtreebooks.com

Created by Bobbie Kalman

Dedicated by Rose Gowsell
For my pin-pal, Nico Tripodi – Love Godmother Rosie

Editor-in-Chief
Bobbie Kalman

Writing team
Niki Walker
Sarah Dann

Editorial director
Niki Walker

Project editors
Laura Hysert
Rebecca Sjonger

Editors
John Crossingham
Amanda Bishop

Copy editors
Molly Aloian
Kathryn Smithyman

Art director
Robert MacGregor

Design
Rose Gowsell

Production coordinator
Heather Fitzpatrick

Photo research
Laura Hysert

Special thanks to
Kelsey Halagian; Jordan Halagian; Melody and Mark Halagian;
Rebecca McInerney; Brian McInerney; Bob and Deborah McInerney;
Victoria Arsenault; Aaron Arsenault; Robert Kent; Robert Hutchings;
Andy Frampton; William Frampton; Tyler Hendry; Alex Fraser;
Rob Langelaan and Jo-Ellen White, Fairview Bowling Lanes;
Joyce Jocham, Publications Manager, Young American Bowling Alliance

Consultants
Cary Pon, Manager of Coach Development and Certification,
 USA Bowling Coaching
Mark Miller, Publications Manager, Bowling Headquarters
Hugh Hendry, Manager, Bowlerama Kennedy

Photographs
Marc Crabtree: pages 1, 3, 4, 5, 8, 9, 12, 14, 15, 16, 18, 20,
21, 22, 23, 24, 26, 27, 28, 29
All other images by PhotoDisc

Illustrations
All illustrations by Bonna Rouse except the following:
Katherine Kantor: pages 13 (top), 16, 17, 19, 29, 31
Trevor Morgan: page 9 (bottom)
Rose Gowsell: page 25

Crabtree Publishing Company

www.crabtreebooks.com   1-800-387-7650

PMB 16A	612 Welland Avenue	73 Lime Walk
350 Fifth Avenue	St. Catharines	Headington
Suite 3308	Ontario	Oxford
New York, NY	Canada	OX3 7AD
10118	L2M 5V6	United Kingdom

Cataloging-in-Publication Data
Walker, Niki
 Bowling in action / Niki Walker & Sarah Dann;
photographs by Marc Crabtree.
       p. cm. -- (The sports in action series)
Includes index.
Offers a brief introduction to the history, techniques, equipment,
and rules of bowling, both five- and ten-pin.
  ISBN 0-7787-0335-5 (RLB) -- ISBN 0-7787-0355-X (pbk.)
  1. Bowling--Juvenile literature. [1. Bowling.] I. Dann, Sarah.
II. Crabtree, Marc, ill. III. Title. IV. Series: Sports in action.
GV903.5.W35 2003
794.6--dc21
                                                      2003001833
                                                           LC

Contents

What is bowling?

Bowling is a sport in which players **bowl**, or roll, a ball at a target. More than 100 million people play this game! Bowling is popular because people of any size, strength, or age can bowl. Bowling is also challenging. It requires good aim, **hand-eye coordination**, and technique.

In **pin games**, players try to knock over a group of upright wooden targets called **pins**. **Tenpin** and **fivepin** are both types of pin bowling. Fivepin is played mainly in Canada. Tenpin bowling, however, is popular all over the world. This book covers the basic skills you need for tenpin bowling.

Bowling through history

People have played bowling games for thousands of years. Historians believe that ancient Egyptians may have played a version of the game as early as 5200 B.C.E. Since then, bowling games have spread around the world. Today's tenpin game became common in the United States in the late 1800s. Bowling became especially popular in the 1950s, when television networks began broadcasting tenpin **tournaments**, or competitions. Today, millions of people still watch bowling tournaments on TV. Bowling organizations hope that the game will someday become an Olympic sport.

Let's go bowling!

There are many ways to enjoy bowling. You can play with friends for fun, or you can join a **league** and bowl competitively against other members. Many bowling centers organize junior leagues and tournaments on weekends. You can choose to bowl as an individual or as part of a team.

*Working with a coach is a great way to improve your bowling skills. You can develop your own style by becoming familiar with the **swing** and the **footwork** required to bowl the ball smoothly.*

Welcome to the lanes

People play tenpin bowling on a long wooden surface called a **lane**. Lanes are usually located in buildings known as bowling centers. Most centers have several lanes as well as areas for players to sit, keep score, select balls, rent shoes, and buy snacks. You will share the center with other bowlers, so it is important to practice proper **etiquette**, or manners, and show respect for other bowlers.

Here are some general rules to keep in mind:

- Do not drop or throw the ball.
- Stay behind the **foul line** at all times.
- Be quiet when other players are taking their turns.
- Always wear proper bowling shoes on the lane.
- Keep food and drinks away from the lane.

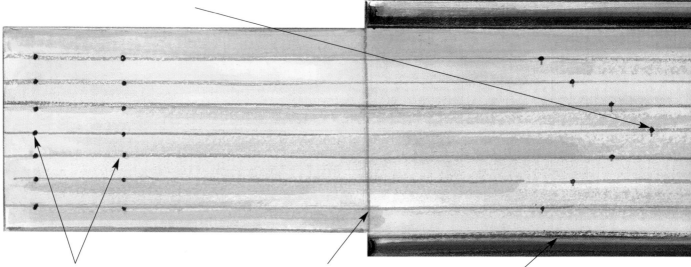

Locator dots and *arrows* help you aim at the pins as you bowl the ball.

The **approach** is marked with dots to help you set up your feet and aim your shot as you bowl the ball.

You must let go of the ball as your foot reaches the foul line. If your foot crosses the foul line, you don't score any points, no matter how many pins you knock down.

The **channel** is a deep groove on either side of the lane. It catches balls that roll off the lane. A ball in the channel can't hit any pins, and the bowler does not score any points. The channel used to be called the gutter.

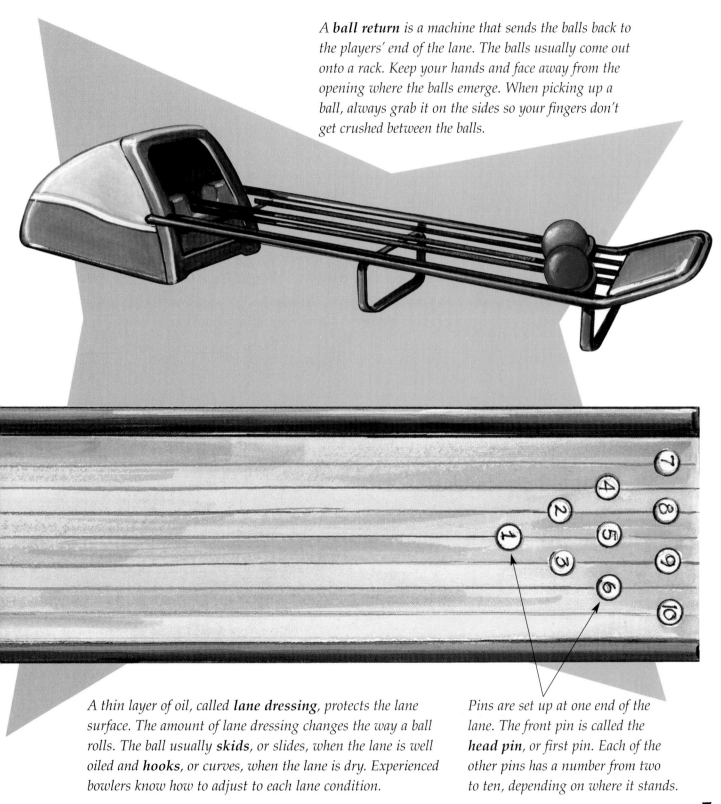

A **ball return** is a machine that sends the balls back to the players' end of the lane. The balls usually come out onto a rack. Keep your hands and face away from the opening where the balls emerge. When picking up a ball, always grab it on the sides so your fingers don't get crushed between the balls.

A thin layer of oil, called **lane dressing**, protects the lane surface. The amount of lane dressing changes the way a ball rolls. The ball usually **skids**, or slides, when the lane is well oiled and **hooks**, or curves, when the lane is dry. Experienced bowlers know how to adjust to each lane condition.

Pins are set up at one end of the lane. The front pin is called the **head pin**, or first pin. Each of the other pins has a number from two to ten, depending on where it stands.

7

The essentials

Most of the equipment you need for bowling can be found at a bowling center. The pins and balls are included in the cost of renting the lane. You can rent bowling shoes if you don't have a pair of your own. If you bowl often, you may want to buy your own ball and shoes. Buying your own equipment allows you to get the best fit. If you have your own equipment, you'll need a bowling bag to carry it to and from the center.

Wear clothing that is loose enough to allow you to move easily. Your arms will be able to swing freely in shirts with loose sleeves.

Bowling shoes have smooth leather soles that help you slide on the balls of your feet as you bowl the ball. Rubber heels grip the lane when you walk so you won't fall. You must wear bowling shoes on the lane.

All about the ball

The most important piece of equipment is your bowling ball. All tenpin balls are the same size—27 inches (68.5 cm) around. They can weigh anywhere from six to sixteen pounds (2.7-7.2 kg). The balls have three holes drilled into them. One hole is for your thumb, and the other two are for your middle finger and ring finger. The holes in **house balls**, or balls that belong to the center, are drilled to fit the fingers of most bowlers. Heavy balls usually have large holes, since larger players tend to use them. Lighter balls have smaller holes because bowlers with small fingers usually use them. Before you start bowling, be sure the holes fit your fingers comfortably and the ball is not too heavy for you to swing.

finger holes

thumb hole

Test a ball's weight by holding it straight out in front of you. You should be able to hold it steady for five seconds. If it's too heavy, try a lighter ball.

Lane dressing can build up on balls. Players use alcohol to clean and protect their balls between games. Most players wipe them with a soft towel before each shot.

Your thumb should fit all the way into the thumb hole. Your fingers need to go into the holes only as far as your second knuckles. As you become a better bowler, your fingers may go only as far as the first knuckle.

When bowling, your body can lose moisture. Bowling centers often have many kinds of beverages available, but water is the best choice for replacing your body's lost moisture.

9

Warming up

Bowling tests your strength and challenges your coordination. You use most of the muscles in your body to stay balanced as you bowl the ball. You can reduce your chances of injury by warming up your muscles before you play. Warm up for about five minutes with a brisk walk and then do the exercises shown on these pages. They help loosen up the muscles you use most as you bowl. Remember to breathe normally as you hold the stretches.

neck stretch

It is easy to hurt your neck, so do this stretch carefully. Tilt your head forward to lower your chin to your chest. Slowly roll your head toward one shoulder and then back to the other shoulder. Do not roll your head farther than feels comfortable and never roll your head backward.

Lunges

Stand with your feet hip-distance apart. Take a big step forward with your left leg. When you land, make sure your left knee is directly over your ankle. Bend your right knee so that your right heel lifts off the ground. Keep your hips forward. With your left leg, push yourself back to the starting position. Repeat the lunge with your right leg forward. Do ten lunges for each side.

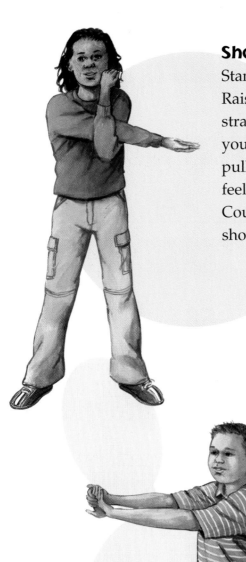

Shoulder stretch

Stand up straight with your shoulders relaxed. Raise your right arm in front of you, keeping it straight. Bring your left arm underneath it, so that your arms meet at the elbows. Use your left arm to pull your right arm gently across your body. You'll feel a stretch in the back of your right shoulder. Count to ten. Release your arms, relax your shoulders, and then stretch the other shoulder.

Side stretch

Stand with your feet shoulder-width apart. Reach up with your right hand and reach down with your left hand, stretching both arms straight. Lean slightly to your left until you feel the muscles stretching in your right side. Repeat the stretch with your left arm up. Hold the stretch for ten seconds on each side.

Stop signs

Reach your left arm straight out in front of you, as if you're motioning for someone to stop. With your right hand, gently pull back the fingers on your left hand until you feel a stretch in your wrist. Do five stretches for each wrist.

The aim game

*Planning and **executing**, or completing, your shots takes concentration and confidence. Try to **visualize**, or picture, the end result of the shot in your mind.*

Each time it's your turn to bowl, you get two chances to knock down as many pins as you can. You score a point for each pin that falls. If you knock down all ten pins with your first ball, it's called a **strike**. If you knock down all the pins using two balls, it's called a **spare**. To bowl strikes and spares, you need to have excellent aim. You'll also need to be able to roll the ball with some force and know how to **deflect**, or knock, pins into one another. As you get more experienced, you'll learn how to make the ball travel along different paths toward the pins, improving your game even more.

Target bowling

When you step up to the lane for the first time, you'll realize that the pins are quite a distance away! It's difficult to aim your shot at a target that's so far away. Luckily, the locator arrows give you a closer target. The arrows line up with the front pins. Aiming at the center arrow will help you hit the head pin. If you use the arrows on either side of the center arrow, you can aim at the pins on either side of the head pin.

The pocket

With your first ball, you should aim for the **pocket**. For right-handed bowlers, the pocket is between the first and third pins. For left-handed bowlers, the pocket is between the first and second pins. To hit the pocket, aim for the second or third arrow from the middle. Slide your foot in line with the center dot on the floor, but don't go over the foul line.

left-handed bowlers' pocket

right-handed bowlers' pocket

Entry angle

You can make the ball travel straight or in a curved path. A **straight ball** rolls in a straight line from the point you release it to the pins. It hits the pins straight on. A **curved** or **hook ball** follows a curved path, rolling toward the channel and then back toward the pins.

It rolls into the pins at a steep angle. The angle at which the ball hits the pins is called the **entry angle**. Because of its entry angle, a hook ball hits and knocks down more pins than a straight ball does. Turn to pages 16-17 to read more about how to make these shots.

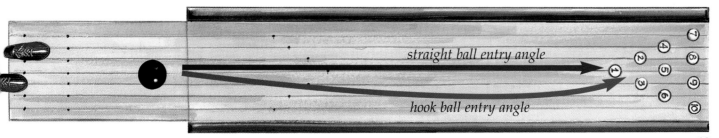

straight ball entry angle

hook ball entry angle

Bowling the ball

Swinging and rolling a bowling ball smoothly and with control takes balance and coordination. The instructions in this book are for right-handed bowlers. If you are left-handed, switch "right" and "left" in the instructions.

The most common set of steps for **delivering**, or preparing to roll the ball, is the **four-step delivery**. You take four strides to reach the foul line and then **release**, or let go of, the ball, as shown below.

Stance

The **stance** is the way you stand as you prepare your shot. Aim your shot and position your feet along the first row of locator dots. Grip the ball with your right hand and support it in front of you with your left hand. Stand with your feet slightly apart and your knees bent for balance.

Pushaway

Take a step with your right foot. As you step, raise your arms and straighten them toward the pins. This move is called the **pushaway**. The ball should be above your waist but below your shoulder. Keep the ball slightly to your side and continue to support it with your left hand.

Midswing

Take a step forward with your left foot and let the ball drop downward at your side. Take your left hand off the ball and let your right arm and the ball swing back freely. This move is called the **midswing**.

Fancy footwork

It can be tricky trying to perfect your footwork and swing at the same time. Try practicing the footwork by itself at first. Move through the steps over and over again until you can do them without thinking. The size of your steps should increase as you move from the first to the fourth step. The power of your roll is created with your legs and the speed of your body—not with your arms.

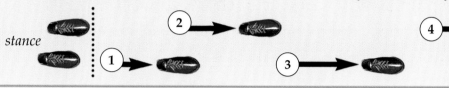

Backswing

*Extend your left arm away from your body for balance. As you step forward with your right foot, continue swinging the ball backward. The ball reaches the highest point of the **backswing** at the end of the step.*

Release

*As you step forward with your left foot, swing the ball forward. Your toes should land just before the foul line. Bend the your left knee and stretch your right leg behind you for balance. Release the ball as it passes your left foot. **Follow through**, or continue swinging your right arm up until it is about forehead height.*

15

The right release

Being able to bowl straight balls and hook balls with control prepares you for any situation in your game. The delivery is the same for both these shots, but the release is different.

Letting go

As you release the ball, your fingers need to make the ball **lift** and **spin**, or rotate. Together, lift and spin make the ball roll smoothly instead of skidding down the lane. You cause lift when you follow through. You create spin with your release. As you release the ball, your thumb should **clear**, or leave, its hole first. Your fingers then clear their holes. Just before they do, **squeeze**, or curl your fingers toward your wrist. Your palm should face the ceiling.

Send it straight

Straight balls are accurate and good for knocking down one pin at a time. You'll use a straight ball to clean up leftover pins. This shot should be your most reliable one. You will use it often to bowl spares (see pages 18-19).

To bowl a straight ball, release the ball with the palm of your hand behind it, facing the pins.

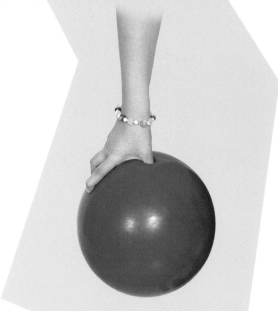

To bowl a hook ball, release the ball with your palm facing you rather than the pins. Twist your wrist to this position as you near the end of your delivery.

The hook ball

A hook ball is the best choice for your first shot. It's the surest way to bowl a strike. When a hook ball hits the pocket, it knocks down the first, third, fifth, and ninth pins. These pins fall and knock down the pins around them, as shown right. Often, all the pins fall and you bowl a strike. Using a straight ball for your first shot will knock down only the first, second, and third pins (far right). The weight of the pins deflects the ball and stops it from hitting any other pins.

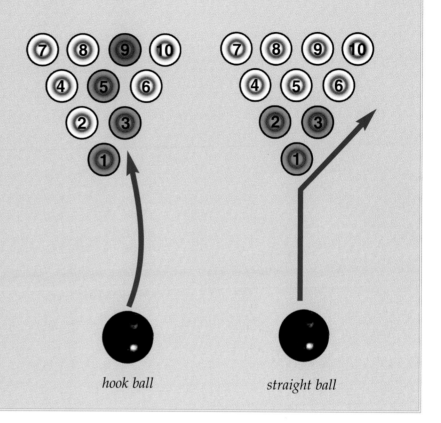

hook ball   *straight ball*

Spare me

Bowling strikes is difficult, but bowling spares can be even harder. To get a spare, you have to aim at specific pins left over from your first ball and knock them down with a single shot. The leftover pins are called the **spare leave**. There are more than 250 possible **spare-leave combinations**. Some of them are much easier to **convert**, or make into spares, than others are.

Splits are the pits

When the spare leave has pins that aren't next to one another, it's called a **split**. Splits are very difficult to convert. To convert a split, you need to aim your shot to deflect some of the pins into the rest. You have to hit the pins at just the right angle to send them flying in the direction of the other pins.

Spare shooting

When trying for a spare, always aim for one of the **target pins**, shown right. Sometimes the target pin you're aiming for may not even be there! Aiming where the pin once stood can still help you knock down the rest of the pins. Here are some general rules for bowling spares:

- If the spare leave is on the inside of the lane, aim the ball at the outside edges of the pins.

- If the spare leave is on the outside of the lane, aim for the inside edges of the pins.

- If the spare leave is in the middle, bowl the ball straight down the center of the lane.

Target pins

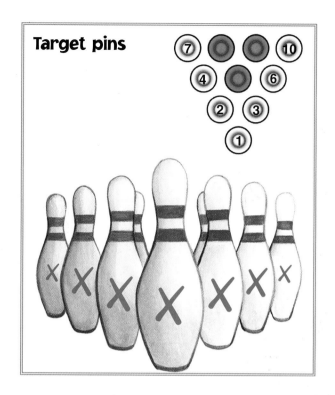

Bed post

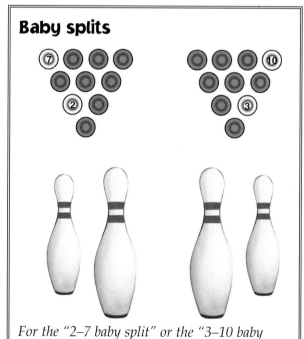

The bed post is one of the most common splits in bowling. It is usually left when the first ball hits the head pin directly. To convert this spare, aim inside the 6 pin and try to deflect the ball into the 4 pin. The 6 pin will knock the 10, and the 4 will hit the 7.

Baby splits

For the "2–7 baby split" or the "3–10 baby split," target the missing 4 or 6 pins. Aiming for the missing 4 or 6 pins will send the ball between the two remaining pins, knocking them down.

Making improvements

There is only one way to become a better bowler—practice! On the next four pages, you'll find tips to make the most of your practice time. The swing-and-slide drill below helps you perfect one of the most important skills in bowling—the delivery. It's a good idea to practice your delivery with a coach or partner, so he or she can watch your movements and offer tips on how to improve. If you don't have a coach or partner, practice in front of a mirror. When you are comfortable with each of the four stages, put them all together and work on developing a smooth flow from start to finish.

Swing-and-slide

Practice the swing-and-slide drill to perfect your delivery. For the pushaway, your right hand should be between your waist and shoulder in height, and not too close or too far away from your body.

Swing your right arm back for the backswing. Your right hand should be just above your waist and not behind your back. Look in a mirror or ask a friend if your backswing is ending up in the right spot. If it's not, keep practicing!

As you move your right arm forward for the release, slide your left leg forward as well. Remember to bend your knee as you finish the release. Practice this drill until you can perform the pushaway, backswing, and release correctly and in one fluid motion.

Improve your backswing

This bowler's backswing is too far behind his body. He will not be able to swing smoothly.

For the ball to swing freely, it needs to start directly behind his right shoulder.

Improve your release

This bowler is leaning too far forward on her release, which will shorten her slide and decrease the speed of her shot. She will also have a hard time hitting the target.

She needs to keep her body upright and hold the position, even after her release. Holding this finish position will improve her balance as she releases the ball.

Practice tips

Even after you understand how your delivery, release, and aim will knock down the pins, you won't bowl strikes and spares every time. It takes time and effort to get your body to bowl the ball the way you want it to! The best way to improve your game is to practice aiming at targets. Pick one pin or space and aim for it over and over again. Watch your target all the way through your shot.

Hit the pocket

The most important target to hit is the pocket (see page 13). Start every practice by trying to hit the pocket ten times in a row. Work on making the correct entry angle as you practice your hook ball. The correct angle will knock down the 1, 3, 5, and 9 pins. Use your straight ball to clean up any pins left over from your hook shot.

Hit the target pins

Another great exercise is to aim for each of the target pins, one at a time. Start with the 7 pin and work around the triangle to the 10 pin. Try to hit each target pin three times.

When possible, bring along a coach or a friend who knows about bowling. Ask him or her to look closely at your delivery, footwork, and release. Ask him or her to tell you what you are doing wrong. Try to correct your moves as you go.

Having trouble?

It takes a while to get the hang of bowling. Try using the tips on this page to correct common problems. Practice the moves with your coach or a partner until you can do them with ease.

No power

If you're having trouble hitting the pins hard enough, your ball may be too heavy (see page 9). A heavy ball is hard to deliver well. You should also check your knee bend and practice your slide to get power behind your shot.

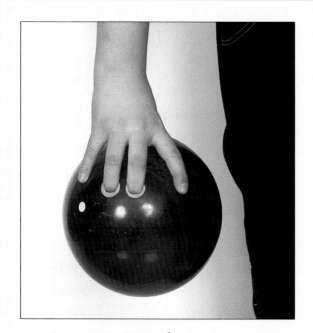

Can't reach the pins

If the ball doesn't even reach the pins but ends up in the channel, you probably need to practice squeezing your fingers as you release the ball (see page 16). Without squeeze, the shot has little power and the ball will roll off to one side. Make sure you don't keep your thumb in the hole too long, or your fingers won't be able to lift and spin the ball properly.

Off to one side

If you consistently bowl the ball too far to one side, you may be holding on to the ball too long before you release it. A late release pulls the ball across your body and sends it across the lane. Practice swinging in front of a mirror to be sure your swing is straight.

Keeping score

A bowling game is made up of ten **frames**, or turns. For each frame, a bowler gets two chances to knock down all the pins. The bowler gets one point for each pin knocked down. Spares and strikes are scored a little differently. When you bowl a spare, you score ten points plus the points from the first ball of your next frame. When you get a strike, you score ten points plus the points from your next two balls. You can score up to 30 points in each frame. A **perfect game** is one in which a bowler gets a strike with every ball. It has a score of 300 points. You need to practice your skills a lot before you can bowl a perfect game!

Who wins?

Keeping score can be confusing at first. Luckily, most bowling centers have **automatic scoring**, which means computers keep score for you. You should still learn how to keep score, however, so that you can plan shots and understand the game.

*Bowling centers often provide **scorecards** such as the one on the next page. Bowlers use them to keep track of their scores. Many centers, however, use computers to help bowlers keep score, as shown above. Computerized scoring helps keep the game moving quickly.*

The number of pins you knock down on your second shot is recorded in the small box.

Strikes are marked with an X in the small box.

The number of pins you knock down on your first ball is recorded to the left of the small box.

The total number of points for the game so far is recorded at the bottom of the box. Points are added to the total from the last turn so you can keep track of your overall score as you bowl from frame to frame.

If you don't knock down any pins, you mark the miss with a horizontal dash.

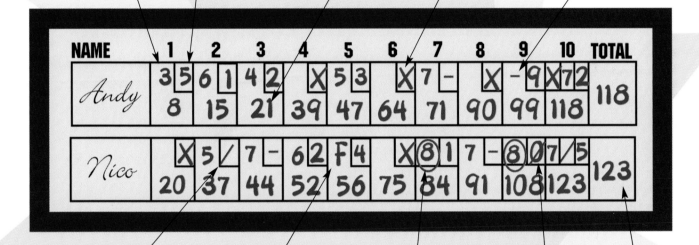

Spares are marked with a diagonal slash across the small box.

Fouls are marked with an F. If you foul on the first ball, you reset all ten pins and get one more ball.

Mark a split with a circle around the number of pins you knock over. Players keep track of splits to see how well they're bowling. Splits don't change the scoring.

The final score is recorded in the total box. The player with the highest score wins.

If you manage to score a spare from a split, it is called a **spared split**. Mark it with a circle with a diagonal slash through it. Count it as a spare.

League play

A lot of people bowl just for fun, but many also bowl in leagues and tournaments. Competitions are set up either for teams of bowlers or for **singles**, or individual bowlers, to play against one another. Some tournaments have competitors from the same bowling center. Others feature bowlers from different centers, cities, or even from other states. Tournaments are held all around the world.

Tournament players wear team shirts. Teammates encourage one another and help plan strategies for their shots.

Types of tournaments

Bowling centers run various kinds of tournaments. The tournaments differ in how they calculate bowlers' scores. In **scratch tournaments**, the winner is the bowler with the highest score for a game. In a **handicap tournament**, bowlers' average scores are calculated for the season. Bowlers with lower average scores are given a **handicap**, or extra points, before the game even starts. The handicap gives them a better chance against bowlers with higher averages. For team bowling, the entire team's average score is calculated, and the team with the lower average gets a handicap. In **bracket tournaments**, bowlers compete only against others with averages close to their own.

*In **scotch doubles**, two players make up a team. They take turns bowling on the same lane—one bowls the first shot and the other cleans up. Partners take turns taking the first shot.*

Calculating your handicap

1. Add total points for season:

145 + 196 + 202 + 221 = 764

2. Divide by number of games played:

764 ÷ 4 games = 191

3. Subtract average from your league's target score:

200 - 191 = 9

4. Multiply by 0.9:

9 × 0.9 = 8.1 or 8

Handicap = 8

What's your handicap?

To calculate your handicap, you first have to figure out your average. Add up the total number of points you've scored all season and divide that by the number of games you have played. The number you get is your average. Subtract your average from your league's **target score**. This target is often set at 200. Depending on your league, your handicap will be between 70% and 100% of the difference between your average and the target score. Many leagues use 90% handicaps. To calculate a 90% handicap, multiply the difference between your average and the target score by 90%, or 0.9. The number you get is your handicap.

Fivepin bowling

Fivepin bowling pins and balls are smaller and lighter than those used in tenpin bowling. There are no finger holes drilled into fivepin balls. They are small enough for players to hold in the palms of their hands. A bowler's swing and delivery in fivepin bowling are similar to those in tenpin bowling. The release is slightly different, however. Since there are no holes in the ball, fivepin bowlers turn their wrists as they release the balls to make them hook.

Fivepin balls are small enough to hold in the palm of one hand.

The birth of fivepin

Fivepin bowling started in Toronto, Canada, in 1909. Some bowlers at a tenpin center found the balls too heavy to control. The center's owner cut down some tenpins, set up a smaller lane, and made a smaller ball for these customers. Fivepin bowling caught on quickly. Today, the sport is as popular in Canada as tenpin bowling is.

When bowling a fivepin ball, keep your palm facing the pins to make a straight ball.

Scoring fivepin

In fivepin, different pins are worth different numbers of points. The **king pin**, or front pin, is worth five points, the middle pins are worth three points, and the outside pins are worth two points. Players bowl ten frames, with three balls per frame. Each frame is worth a maximum of forty-five points, and a perfect game is 450 points.

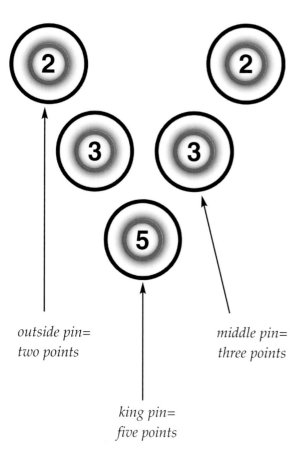

outside pin=
two points

middle pin=
three points

king pin=
five points

Fivepin bowling is especially popular with young or beginner bowlers because the balls are easy to hold and deliver.

Other bowling games

Bowling games are played in over 90 countries. There are many versions of bowling around the world. Some are similar to tenpin bowling. **Candlepin** bowlers use smaller balls than those used in fivepin bowling, and the pins are slimmer, resembling candles. In **duckpin** bowling, the ball and pins are smaller than those used in other games. The pins are circled with bands of hard rubber that send them flying when they are hit.

Target bowling games such as **bocce**, **lawn bowling**, and **carpet bowling**, are also popular. In target bowling, players score points by throwing or rolling balls as close to a target as possible. Many of the oldest bowling games are forms of target bowling. Like pin bowling, target bowling games require aim, skill, and coordination. They can be played in leagues or just for fun. They require little equipment and setup when you're playing for fun.

In bocce, the player who throws his or her ball closest to the small target ball scores a point. Sometimes the game is so close, players must use a measuring tape to figure out who wins!

Bocce

Bocce is the oldest known version of bowling. This Italian game has spread around the world. Bocce uses a small ball as a target instead of pins. The target ball is tossed onto a sand or grass pit. Players throw their balls as close to the small ball as possible. The ball closest to the small ball scores a point.

Lawn bowling is a popular sport among players of all ages.

Lawn bowling

Some of the oldest sports clubs in North America began as lawn bowling clubs. Lawn bowling is played on closely cropped grass lanes. A small white ball, called a **jack**, is rolled on the lane. Bowlers roll their balls as close to the jack as possible. The balls used in lawn bowling are covered in leather and are slightly **warped**, or bent. This shape makes the balls curve as they roll.

Carpet bowling is a version of lawn bowling that is played indoors on carpet instead of on grass. Carpet bowling tournaments happen all across the United States and Canada.

Glossary

Note: Boldfaced words that are defined in the book may not appear in the glossary.

backswing The movement of the ball behind the body with the arm straightened

delivery The preparation to roll the ball

footwork The placement and movement of the feet

foul line The line at the edge of a bowling lane that a player's foot must not cross

frame One of ten turns that make up a game

hand-eye coordination Combining what you see with smooth hand movements

league A group of people who compete with one another and with other leagues

lift A movement that makes the ball skim lightly along the lane's surface

release To let go of the ball after a swing

spare The act of knocking down all ten pins using two balls

spare-leave combination An arrangement of pins left standing after the first ball

spin A movement that makes the ball rotate as it travels down the lane

split An arrangement in which the leftover pins are not standing next to one another

strike The act of knocking down all ten pins with the first ball

swing The movement of an arm as it arcs and releases the ball

target pin A pin at which players aim because it will likely knock over other pins

target score A score against which individual players measure their average score

Index

1 2 3 4 5 6 7 8 9 0 Printed in the U.S.A. 2 1 0 9 8 7 6 5 4 3